The Zombie Economy

Includes lost in the fog

S. E. McKenzie

S. E. MCKENZIE

ZOMBIE ECONOMY and Lost in the Fog

DEDICATION
To everyone who has been left out in the cold.

S. E. MCKENZIE

This book is a book of speculative fiction. Characters, companies, governments, places, events, are either products of the author's imagination or used fictitiously. Any resemblance to persons (living or dead), companies, governments, places and/or events, is a coincidence.

ZOMBIE ECONOMY and Lost in the Fog

TABLE OF CONTENTS

S. E. MCKENZIE

ZOMBIE ECONOMY and Lost in the Fog

S. E. MCKENZIE

ZOMBIE ECONOMY

I

The invisible hand
Was holding yours all day
It didn't matter

You had no money to pay
So no one cared what you had to say
And the sun never shined

For you, Drew
And every day is a day of dread
Many think they would be better off dead.

II

Paper comes from a dead tree
But still in theory more worthy than you
So what can you do?

ZOMBIE ECONOMY and Lost in the Fog

III

The visible feet
Walk up and down the street
As they move around the homeless

Sometimes the visible feet walk in a line
Sometimes slow
Sometimes fast

IV

And those with visible feet
Buy what they can to eat
Everything else is secondary

Cause surviving is the law of the beast
All connected on this food chain
That feeds our marrow

Even though this path is narrow
It is a step which must be taken
To start the game

S. E. MCKENZIE

Of Sum Zero
One can win so big
One forgets

Who you are
When you lose it all
Your feet will be still on the street

Now so mean
A place that you have never seen
People living inside cardboard boxes

As you are held back, they will condescend
Still you must feed your marrow
On this path of greed so narrow

One must climb above it all
For one side will fall in the end
One side wins at such expense to the other,

And one way or another
You will be watched by big brother
In this prison town

ZOMBIE ECONOMY and Lost in the Fog

V
Can't you see?
How this zombie economy
Shapes you and me

Fear destroys creation and innovation
Speed ups recession
Before you slump into depression

Panhandler is really a cop in disguise
Looks in the window of your car
So he can win a prize

One way or another
He is your big brother
Trying to catch you holding your phone

He gives out tickets
The faceless and nameless brand.
Is he part of the invisible hand?

S. E. MCKENZIE

VI

Big brother gives you a ticket
Now you have no money for food
But one way or another

He is your big brother.

Hey Drew, what will you do?
You have a brave smile
Will only last a while

Until you get kicked down by the gatekeeper
One way or another he is your big brother
Though he does not know your name

To him everyone is the same
The strange combination of natural law and artificial
selection
Leads to advanced sadness and depression

ZOMBIE ECONOMY and Lost in the Fog

See all these fishes and loaves
Piled high by the mount
To share

When Peter could not be robbed to pay Paul
Market failure was felt by all
When the walls come falling down

Some won't mind
Others without walls will grow to be unkind
Others will close their eyes in fright

And hope to be comforted all night
In the glow of hope
Others will narrow their scope

For it is the way
Of the zombie economy
To ignore the chaos

The police state tried to control
The mounting loss
This made the masses cross

S. E. MCKENZIE

VII

As the visible feet
Kept walking on the street
Many of those feet began to disappear

There was so much doubt
And a growing climate of fear
Both far and near

And Drew's Momma said
Where are you Drew?
You should be in bed

Drew knew too
And his head was filled with dread
Couldn't get his foot in the door

To enter a future he was prepared for.
The world was on the brink of war
So Drew gave up too.

ZOMBIE ECONOMY and Lost in the Fog

VIII

As panic set in
The wheels of the economy slowed down
People kept their surplus liquid

As supply and demand
Expected the invisible hand
To stroke good fortune in time

The visible feet
Were in recline
As the movement of things

Began to slow down
The zombie economy
Began to tip

Without a life line
Death gained its grip
And the promise was broken

As the pain had awoken

S. E. MCKENZIE

For risk was too high
So money was laid to rest
In jars behind bars and under the bed

Fear of fear and social unrest
Made it harder still
To build a better world

With more opportunity
So many were afraid to make it be
This feeling of doom divided society

There was the bad and the good
The weak and the strong
All hiding in the hood

Still believing that killing was wrong
The movement of things was interrupted
As a man with a gun stood at attention

One way or another he was your big brother

ZOMBIE ECONOMY and Lost in the Fog

Death and fear of it,
Was on everyone's mind.
So why care or be kind?

They all had to ask,
People are only themselves,
When wearing a mask.

The world was full of gloom and doom
Only love could make hope bloom
Paving a path into a kinder way.

And many stopped believing in love
Cause there was just too much scary stuff
There was fright talked about on the news all night

In the zombie way
Half alive and have dead
As debt dangled over your head

But then you drowned your pain
As you were stuck standing in the rain
Waiting your turn and it never came.

S. E. MCKENZIE

IX

The race is fast
Some will drown
Others will last

And win the crown
Some will need a life line
When no safety net is found

Others will be caught up
In red tape
While their visible feet are bound

X

Ride the economy like a bike
Keep your balance
And visible feet moving

Or the economy will crash
In the usual zombie way
And one way or another

Big brother will be watching you

ZOMBIE ECONOMY and Lost in the Fog

XI
See the frown
See the malice in their face
While they bring you down

You must compete until the end
In this place, almost a prison town
Where streets are empty at night

They are that way out of fright
Barriers that block the way
Without any concern for what has been lost.

For this is almost a prison town.
Here you are half alive and half dead,
As the debt load hangs over your head.

In the usual zombie way
You must worry about who is following you?
When they drive around the block and stare at you

And who protects you and me
From this zombie economy
Sealed with degradation, alienation and marginalization?

S. E. MCKENZIE

Easy for them when they can print money
And sell it back to the bank
Giving and taking away life

For that is the usual way
In the Zombie economy
That bites you until you bleed

As you roll on the ground in need
As you beg for your life
To be the best you can be

You are marked by the manmade beast
So he can feast
On your degradation

Half dead and half alive
Few are real
When not wearing a mask

One still must do the task
Needed to keep on living
Just to keep the hope alive

ZOMBIE ECONOMY and Lost in the Fog

A hurt sensation
When a hello would do
Alienation

When there is no love surrounding you.
Half alive and half dead
That is the way in this zombie economy

Can't economize
Only marginalize
But don't let them devalue you

Keep your head high
And one day there will be a better way
With no war and debt to pay for war

No famine or suspicion of the underdog
No more getting followed around the block
Even though one way or another

He is your big brother

S. E. MCKENZIE

Once up in arms
So blind to hypocrisy
In the usual zombie economical way

Giving and taking life

Wastage and cruelty
There was no end
As data flowed it had to bend

Around mountains and through river beds
As debt mounted
The economy was given life while the future could be
ceased.

In the zombie way
They follow a person around the block
But never say hello

Fear ruined innovation
So how could the economy grow?
Only through selling out tomorrow

As ambition froze in fear

ZOMBIE ECONOMY and Lost in the Fog

XII

Visible feet were walking
On one side of the earth
While reclining on the other side

The illuminated were weeping
They had nowhere to hide
Their loss was tremendous

As data moved as fast as it could
Under rivers and over mountains
Data moved like liquid fountains

Dead matter fueled electricity so alive
While only the fittest were meant to survive
Said the one prone to illuminate,

What he said was final

For there was no need to debate
In the circle of the elite
For that would create more data to return

S. E. MCKENZIE

And some said that it was all a trap
The economy had crashed and could not move
While the visible feet kept walking the street

The motion was able to support and energize
As the beat of the skin drum
Was heard far and wide.

"Now what do you see?"
The man asked the bird of steel
The drone was alone

And had nothing to say
Someone was about to pay
As they toiled for oil all day

The missile flew into the air
Some said it was not fair
Others needed a sign

So they could feel free to care

ZOMBIE ECONOMY and Lost in the Fog

As data was able to bend
There seemed to be no end
To how prices could fluctuate

Bottom out
Then bounce back
Like a dead cat

With nine lives
But none to spare
For there were missiles in the air

As money for a moment stood still
The crash was just for a few moments away in time
As value of money fell

Prices began to climb
For some this was heaven
For others it was hell

XIII

How far away did you get
From the paper phantom of debt?
Did you fly away in your jet?

S. E. MCKENZIE

Was it ever really a safe bet
As data flew under river beds
And through tunnels of stone

The faster the trade
Higher the price
Before it fell

Into a manmade hell

Even though the ice
Was now liquid
And could flow freely

Many felt the gloom of doom
For one way or another
The man who was your big brother

Was still watching you
So how could you feel free
To be yourself?

ZOMBIE ECONOMY and Lost in the Fog

Panic stricken
The visible feet ran out of the door
There were more and more

They all ran so fast
No one knew when the fear would end
Fear grew as the walls were falling down

We knew love gave us some strength
When everything around us
Seemed to vanish in thin air

When you have nothing
No one will care
Hey Drew

What will you do?

S. E. MCKENZIE

XIV
Fly the economy like a kite
Above all this bad and sad
Atmosphere

That is what you must do Drew
Before the game ruins you
With one zero to your name

Above the sky line
That you never see
That is where the zombie economy

Rests in food chains
So heavy and strong
And where whatever you do to survive

Can never be wrong.

THE END

Lost In The Fog

S. E. McKenzie

S. E. MCKENZIE

LOST IN THE FOG
I

I heard Mark Bow screaming,
No, I was not dreaming.
For he was begging for mercy

Hoping that the king would hear
For the king was always out of sight,
So Mark Bow begged with all his might.

Even as the sun
Was setting
He never stopped begging.

He begged for mercy
All through the night,
But the king did not hear a word;

Mark Bow did not have that right.

Even though
Mark Bow
Was not yet dead.

ZOMBIE ECONOMY and Lost in the Fog

And Mark Bow said:

"Please dear King
Give the command
And free me from this tree,

So that I can return
To my true love,
My beautiful Marie.

Yes, I missed roll call,
That is very true
But I never would have deserted

A kind king like you."

II
In days gone past

He rode as fast
As his horse Charge
Could trot

S. E. MCKENZIE

For the dead were lying
All around
Their bodies were left to rot.

As their spirits were floating away,

I heard Mark Bow say:
"I have been just one of many
Lost at sea that day,

I should have been more aware,
And I am sorry for this fault.
The fog spread through the sky,

While torrents rained angrily,
I was being rocked
In the arms of my true love

My beautiful Marie.

ZOMBIE ECONOMY and Lost in the Fog

The waves too rocked my ship
So how was I to know
That my ship had been carried

So far away from shore,
While I was sleeping peacefully
Upon the ship's floor,

With my beautiful Marie?

Please kind King
Free me from this tree,
I am not your enemy,

For I was freely giving
My loyalty to you every day,
And I know you will miss my servitude

If you let me die this way.

So don't let me die this way!

You see, I must be free,
To return to my true love,
My beautiful Marie.

S. E. MCKENZIE

III

I have crossed the line
Between Heaven and Earth
Many times for you, dear King

So please give out the command
Which could free me
From this tree,

For I carry this ring
Meant for the hand
Of my true love

My beautiful Marie.

A promise is made to keep,
So don't let me die this way,
For I must return as soon as I can

To my beautiful Marie.

My true love is willing and living,
So I have never been less ready to die;
I force my will to keep my weary eyes open,

ZOMBIE ECONOMY and Lost in the Fog

And my heart pounding as I try not to cry,
Though I feel so weak and very sad.
If I didn't believe in this love so grand,

I would let myself fade away
Into the unknown,
Because I feel so bad.

Somewhere between
Heaven and Earth
I hang here from this tree,
Hoping the force of your crown,
Can set me free,
Without letting me down;

So that I can follow my chosen path
Into tomorrow
With my true love by my side."

And the king did not know Mark Bow
For Mark Bow was the same
As any other man with any other name.

S. E. MCKENZIE

Even though many men said
That the king's days
Were numbered

The king denied feeding off the poor
And said that he was just the same
As other kings ruling from before.

And many were pushed
Into heaven's revolving door,
Into a world where they would yearn no more.

As the time went by,
Mark Bow's future grew bleaker,
As he grew weaker.

And Mark Bow said:

"I awoke and saw,
Three black birds of prey,
Taking refuge on my ship that day.

They were blown away
By the wind so strong,
Just like me and my beautiful Marie.

ZOMBIE ECONOMY and Lost in the Fog

While the storm grew
And the wind blew
We too were lost at sea.

So please forgive me.

IV

The Earth's power
Surrounded me with mist
And that is the reason why

When my sergeant called out
My name from the list
I was not there to reply.

So my sergeant declared
Me missing
While I was still kissing

S. E. MCKENZIE

My true love
My beautiful Marie.
I just want to say

That going AWOL
Was never part of any plan;
So please kind King

I must believe so I don't fade away
That I will be free
Before I die

And I have already told you why
I need to return
To my true love,

My beautiful Marie.

ZOMBIE ECONOMY and Lost in the Fog

V

As I hang from this tree
I see the clouds above
As I remember my true love,

My beautiful Marie.

I must return to her,
And stay close by her side,
For as long as I am still alive.

So kind King,
Grant me the right to stay living,
Now that I have found a new world

Which is so loving and giving,

And this life should stay mine
So that I may share it
With my true love

My beautiful Marie."

S. E. MCKENZIE

VI
Though Mark Bow was a captain

And never a knight;
He had fought with vigour,
And had never lost a fight.

And then Mark Bow said:
"They say I deserted my post,
And that is not true,

I was lost at sea
With my true love,
My beautiful Marie.

While we were lost in the fog,
Trapped between Heaven and Earth
We lost track of time

Though, it was no fault of mine.
Oh kind King, shed mercy upon me
Don't let me die this way

ZOMBIE ECONOMY and Lost in the Fog

For I did return to shore
With a diamond ring
For my true love

My beautiful Marie."

And then Mark Bow said:
"Oh kind King
Of days gone by,

Please cut me down from this tree.
For I am almost dead,
And I must stay living,

For I promised to wed,
My true love,
My beautiful Marie.

I must return to her
For my life is now hers,
Not yours nor mine.

S. E. MCKENZIE

VII

I know Marie is waiting
For the day I can take her hand.
That day could be any day,

Just send out the command."

Then Mark Bow cried out in pain,
Sounding almost insane,
And then he said:

"The Fog sometimes blocks out the light
And can happen any time of day
As the wind blew suddenly

The boat and me and Marie
Drifted away,
And sealed my Fate that day."

And Mark Bow said:
"I returned as soon as I could,
And I did what I should,

So please dear King set me free,

ZOMBIE ECONOMY and Lost in the Fog

So I may return
To my horse and sword,
And my beautiful Marie.

My sword is sharp,
My horse is young,
And I am fit.

So I should be busy
Doing this thing
Called war;

And I would never
Abandon my post,
For my life exists as long

As you remain my willing host.

So dear King, please set me free,
So I may return to my true love,
My beautiful Marie."

S. E. MCKENZIE

VIII
And Mark Bow said:
"I was never born to be
So alone it is true,

I was born to be with
My True Love
My beautiful Marie."

And Mark Bow said:
"Marie was my reason for living
For she was so trusting and forgiving;

And what will I do
Without my true love
Empowering my Soul?

For that love
Would generate
Electricity and energy

ZOMBIE ECONOMY and Lost in the Fog

Whenever I felt faint.

That energy surrounded me,
So deeply and freely,
It astounded me,

Made me feel so free,
Which is why I must return to my true love,
My beautiful Marie.

IX

The war around me
Generates opposing sides,
Both wronged in blood,

Both sides forced to crawl in mud."

X

Then Mark Bow said:
"They say I deserted my post
And that is not true

I was just lost at sea
With my true love,
My beautiful Marie.

S. E. MCKENZIE

And under the stars
The sea trapped us within its tides,
And for a moment we were free from wars,

Until we were swept upon these shores.

XI
Now all the death
Surrounding me
Too sad to see and speak of

Made spirits free
To fly from Earth
Into the Heavens above.

My beautiful Marie.
I will play a melody,
And she will sing along,

And as long as we are together
Our hearty song
Will be hummed in the heavens above for ever."

ZOMBIE ECONOMY and Lost in the Fog

And Mark Bow said:
"I have seen so much sorrow,
And I don't know what to do,

As I walked among the dead,
The fog could see what was really true;
Just like a ghost needing a host to become real.

Just like a ghost

When it is my turn
To rest in eternal sleep,
I hope to keep

My heart music
Pure enough to share,
With my true love,

With nothing left to lose,
The fog will cover broken bones,
With the help of morning dew.

S. E. MCKENZIE

Too many broken hearts
With no beat left to pound,
Fighting men, left all alone

To sleep on this soggy ground.
Why do I go on fighting?
So rich men have a throne.

I am forced to fight this war
While my true love Marie,
Is left crying all alone.

If I had my way,"
I heard Mark Bow say
"I would turn all these weapons

Into plowshares and I would do it right away."

ZOMBIE ECONOMY and Lost in the Fog

XII

And then I heard Mark Bow say

"Fate is not mine to know.
And through my sorrow,
My dreams may appear tomorrow,

Still covered in fog,
Hiding the spectrum of light,
So the rainbow cannot be seen.

XIII

Some wondered where the dead were buried,
Wearing boots as they lay in satin;
The fog was just like a cloud,

Floating above the ground
While the dead
Could not hear a sound;

The skin drum
Kept pounding
Inside me

S. E. MCKENZIE

For this was Life.

XIV
And I was so thankful,

That I had been lost at sea,
With my true love,
My beautiful Marie.

XV
The living awoke
To a new day.
So they arose.

As the fog lingered
All around
Like a ghost

Shadows replaced lives
Now lost in the past
Cursed to float within the will

ZOMBIE ECONOMY and Lost in the Fog

Of those warm currents
As they waved me so gently
I was so glad to know a time

When I was lost at sea,
With my true love,
My beautiful Marie,

Where silent echoes
Of haunted screams
Were hiding in living streams,

And feeding the land
Living water
So tomorrow could grow

If not lost.

XVI

I see the sun come out at last,
The light shines just like a spec,
On what remains, I can't reflect,

S. E. MCKENZIE

For there were not many gains
Earned on this plot of Earth,
Growing further apart from Heaven,

Violence was implied but never shown;
Better that way,
I heard the sergeant say;

If we lie
While they die
They will never know.

So another day went by:
Some laughed,
Some cried,

Some dominated with hate,
And caused a scene
Just to be mean.

And after the instigation:

ZOMBIE ECONOMY and Lost in the Fog

Many died,
While I remembered the days lost at sea
With my true love

My beautiful Marie."

XVII
Hoping for a better day
He knew he had to find
A better way.

As Mark Bow hung in the tree
All he could think of was Marie
And all the times that he would never see;

Mark Bow cried out in his pain
"There is so much to gain
So why must I lose it all?

Without better foresight
For the common man
This kingdom is bound to fall."

S. E. MCKENZIE

XVIII

And Mark Bow said:
"I am so confused
I feel that I have been used.

There are hypocrites
All over the place
And they will trespass on you.

If they can, like a big man,
In a game that only kings
Can win.

My body aches
But never breaks
As far as I can tell;

I am still living somewhere between
Heaven and Earth
And Hell."

And the rainbow
Is seldom seen
Until after the rain

ZOMBIE ECONOMY and Lost in the Fog

So it is hard to explain
Especially when the storm spirit
Appeared so rudely

And swiped me and Marie away
With the force of the tide's sway
Without thought to logistics for my success.

The storm spirit
Changed my fate,
Made me late

For the game where only
Peasant kings can win,
As the sea cursed me in its stormy way.

Now I appear
To have deserted my post,
Though that was never my intent;

I swear
It was never part
Of any plan;

S. E. MCKENZIE

I was only lost at sea
With my true love
My beautiful Marie.

XIX
The ground was covered
With morning dew
So Earth's pain was being soothed too.

As I laid freed
By those angelic birds
That had taken refuge on my ship;

Such noble birds of prey
Pecked at the ropes around my wrists
Until the job was done that day.

And then in the misty rain,
I lay waiting for the sun again.
I laid there so worn and torn,

And I wondered what I had done."

THE END
**ANOTHER S. E. McKENZIE PRODUCTION
(A WORK IN PROGRESS)**

ZOMBIE ECONOMY and Lost in the Fog

S. E. MCKENZIE

Produced by S.E. McKenzie Productions
First Print Edition 2014

ISBN:

Enquiries: 1(778)992-2453
Mailing Address:
S. E. McKenzie Productions
168 B 5th St.
Courtenay, BC
V9N 1J4

Email Address:
messidartha@aol.com

www.ingramcontent.com/pod-product-compliance
Lightning Source LLC
Chambersburg PA
CBHW060539030426
42337CB00021B/4339